HONEY WITH TOBACCO

HONEY

with

TOBACCO

PEG BOYERS

THE UNIVERSITY OF CHICAGO PRESS
Chicago and London

PEG BOYERS is executive editor of *Salmagundi* magazine
and the author of a book of poems titled *Hard Bread*, published
by the University of Chicago Press.

The University of Chicago Press, Chicago 60637
The University of Chicago Press, Ltd., London
© 2007 by The University of Chicago
All rights reserved. Published 2007
Printed in the United States of America

16 15 14 13 12 11 10 09 08 07   1 2 3 4 5

ISBN-13: 978-0-226-06966-1 (cloth)
ISBN-13: 978-0-226-06967-8 (paper)
ISBN-10: 0-226-06966-4 (cloth)
ISBN-10: 0-226-06967-2 (paper)

Library of Congress Cataloging-in-Publication Data

Boyers, Peggy, 1952–
  Honey with tobacco / Peg Boyers.
    p. cm. — (Phoenix poets)
  ISBN-13: 978-0-226-06966-1 (cloth : alk. paper)
  ISBN-10: 0-226-06966-4 (cloth : alk. paper)
  ISBN-13: 978-0-226-06967-8 (pbk. : alk. paper)
  ISBN-10: 0-226-06967-2 (pbk. : alk. paper)
  I. Title.
  PS3602.O94H66 2007
  811'.54—DC22
                        2006020785

⊗ The paper used in this publication meets the minimum
requirements of the American National Standard for
Information Sciences—Permanence of Paper for Printed
Library Materials, ANSI Z39.48-1992.

In memory of John J. O'Higgins (1916–2006)

and

for my mother, María Josefa Lluriá de O'Higgins

and

for my husband, Robert
(always and forever)

Contents

III.

Acknowledgments

Grateful acknowledgment is made to the editors of the following magazines where these poems or versions of these poems first appeared:

Antioch Review: "Lamentation"
Guernica: "Mantilla," "Time Orders Old Age to Destroy Beauty," and "The Effects of Intemperance"
Harvard Review: "Pentecost: Waiting"
New England Review: "Family Portrait"
The New Republic: "Annunciation," reprinted by permission of *The New Republic*, © 2005, The New Republic, LLC.
Notre Dame Review: "Sacra Conversazione" and "Judgment Day"
Ontario Review: "Palm Sunday," "Pietà," and "Catch"
Open City: "Transition: Inheriting Maps"
Paris Review: "Deposition" and "Cup"
Ploughshares: "Bitch Diary"
Raritan: "Before Losing You at the Market, Finding You in the Temple"
Slate: "Abanico Habanero"
Southern Review: "Playa Colorada" and "Tobacco"
Southwest Review: "Agua de Violetas," Volume 84, Number 1, 1998

I am very grateful to the Civitella Ranieri Foundation for its generous support during the preparation of this book and to my indefatigable friends whose tough love throughout this project was essential.

I
HONEY WITH
TOBACCO

La Tuvería or An Earring's Lament

En Cuba tuve—

I'm tired of hearing your complaints.
All that whining about *el exilio*, the tragedy of loss,

In Cuba I had—

the catalogue of things, the status, the riches,
the opulence of it all.

I had a mate. We were a pair. Our mistress was young. We
were young. We would dangle on her ear

Concentrate on what you have.
Forget the past.

and go out on the town. Mojitos at La Floridita,
dancing at the Tropicana and later

No, don't tell me about later.

in the jewel case, an aqua Tiffany box
with white satin interior, we

Tiffany's? From New York? I didn't know you—

would lie together in the pillowy luxury,
my ruby top layer and his aligned, our bases

Please, you needn't—

touching, my diamond waist and his forming a continuous
line. Sometimes we would switch backs, I'd push

I understand that in communities of exile
the population

my piercing needle through his back, his
through mine. That's

tends to lose ground politically as
assimilation takes place, that

how I liked it best, a little harsh, but sweet.
Tu y yo, you and I, is what she called us because our very

longing is a constitutive ingredient
of not only the condition of exile but—

body parts were paired, he and I, forming a single unit, an I and a
thou. Apart

Surely you have adjusted. Look, you're mounted on a ring, you
are independent, and prized. Very attractive for your age, I might add.

we are nothing. Longing doesn't quite—

One adapts?

As to an amputation.

And La Revolución?

Don't make me vomit.

Machine of Regret

I will not turn the crank. No.
Not one revolution
to work the wheel that works the drill that writes the word in stone.

No, I will *not* turn the crank so the wheel pulls
a chain so the hourglass bends
the harrowing will of the harrowing, harrowing harrow-drill.

Give me a simple useless ready-made
hands-off, no complicated contingencies dada
kind of just-kidding regret-gizmo,

the circular plain-old isolate
bicycle wheel,
chaste circle of wanting and getting,

of having, then losing
and having, and wishing
not to have had.

Agua de Violetas

Agua de violetas, eau de violettes,
aroma of infancy, precise
signifier of innocence.

Before taste, smell. Taste can take
you back, but smell drives you home
again, behind the past, under

the remembered image and flavor of it all.
Of course it was in the Tuilleries
that I remembered the violets, the pungence

of daily promenades in sandy afternoons,
nannies gossiping at park benches;
children cleansed, starched, anointed

for the daily exhibition, the ritual of display
and mutual approval. How sweet the smell
of belonging, the confirmation of class.

A Havana variant suffused with violets:
cologne in skinny fluted bottles,
purple splash of release from lessons

and the eternal watch of parental eyes.
Pigeons strutting after corn, the occasional iguana
basking near the hibiscus—spiky but benign.

The vendors' tropical song of *merienda*:
maní, guayava con queso,
batidos de mango, galletas, pirolí.

Refreshment and deception:
the fan palm offers no shade,
the fountain is off limits, and the saccharine

scent of distilled flowers wafts its steamy
gentility over all possible discord, smoothing
mood, soothing tempers

with manners and essence of violets.
Agua de violetas, lost water of a lost world,
I miss your careless dignity.

Once I sampled a scent called
Volupté. I scratched the
folded paper from *The New Yorker*

and sniffed my way back
to Cuba, to the *malecón, el moro,*
El Encanto—

and suddenly there appeared the favorite
Franciscan, the family pederast
out to collect a kiss or more from

a niece, his for the afternoon.
The smell of violets intoxicates him.
Their childish freshness reminds him

of all that he can never retrieve.
If he can just get close enough
to inhale them maybe he'll get back

to the place before he lost his way.
But his breath on her neck
repulses her. She recoils, emits a scream

—a good scream, for she
has practiced it for years in case
such an occasion should arise.

Crying, repentant, he plays
Sousa to distract her, but the brass
and pound only distress her.

She discovers she hates marches,
will always hate marches.
He begs her to keep their secret.

Master now, at seven,
she possesses a certain, precocious
immunity. Her innoculation:

near seduction,
flattery's subtle germ.
That summer

the last of the *agua de violetas*
evaporated. Only the faint scent remained,
a sachet for her lingerie. Such an adult word

for one so young. She waited for her breasts
to grow, shaved her legs, longed hard to menstruate.
Meanwhile, she practiced the flirt, the tease,

and its companion, denial. Also,
the scream.
Agua de mi alma, drink me back.

Tobacco

To rid yourself of envy and sin
mix honey with tobacco.

— CUBAN FOLKSONG

Tabaco, tu boca,
tus bocas—your mouths,
sweet island uncles, your lips

fragrant with Cuban *puros*, and you
lifting me
in a cloud of smoke

for a good-night kiss, passing me,
one to one,
with your dark burly arms

hugging me close so that
my hair, my nightie, take back the smell
to linger over in bed under the mosquito net.

The cousins asleep in rows of cots on the veranda,
the ocean breeze billowing the netting
so it scratches my cheek—the lightest of stings.

Little huddles of white, snug as tobacco hills
swathed in gauze, baking the blonde inner leaves
to wrap, ring with bands and burn.

The sound of Mamita and her sisters singing
—*Quando salí de l'Habana válgame dios*—
Habana puro.

My shallow smoker's breath,
asthmatic, subverts the soul's infant desire,
but the memory of pleasure persists.

Tabaco, tu boca,
tus bocas—Lelén, Pili, Pancho,
and the priest, Benjamín, all the *tíos*

in starched *guayaveras,*
pleats pressed over their stout middles:
tobacco musk of men,

chiefs in a circle, smoking
the weed
like the first *caciques*

Columbus found when he waded to shore
at *Puerto de Mares*, Port of Seas,
Port of Surfs,

Port of Sorrows.
Tabaco. Tu boca—
No se toca.

Tío Cheo, you weren't like the rest. Your
arms were smooth and pink and fine.
And your breath

smelled of *guarapo* when you leaned over
and sang to us
in your pitch perfect voice

American show tunes you'd picked up in college
before the seminary, before
the priesthood, before Uncle Ben

nailed you, took off your frock
and drove you
to Bellevue

where drugs and shock-treatment
dulled away desire.
Too mad now

even for the Franciscans, banished
from their monastery, your habit
repossessed,

you phone from the asylum, asking
for cigarettes: still, at eighty,
craving, unrequited.

Tu boca, Cheo—

Playa Colorada

It was a beach
like all beaches, only perhaps more beautiful.
And the sand was pink not red.

We would arrive in caravans,
hampers overflowing with food and drink
like Aziz and his party on the way to Malabar.

The colonials and their servants away on an outing.
We would stop under thatch umbrellas,
towels and tablecloths spread out against the sea.

My mother in her skirted swim suit
surrounded by fathers of other children,
her olive skin lit through her straw hat.

They would laugh and drink beer
and leer
while the children did the usual beach things,

boring futile tunnels to China, running
at waves and then away,
daring each other to be swallowed.

I would go out by the forbidden rocks and pick off oysters,
then give them to the men to pry open,
cover with lime juice and suck dry.

Once, I saw my mother sucking
an oyster out of another daddy's hand.
Her dappled face bobbed and smiled and her tongue

searched the shell for pearls.

Family Portrait

Puerto La Cruz, 1956

It's the bland fifties but the news
has not reached Venezuela

where the bougainvillea and hibiscus
obscenely bloom.

In our backyard tropical oblivion
the family freezes for the photograph,

and for a millisecond captures falsity
for the record.

Even then you were uncomfortable
out of shadow.

At fourteen your manhood, just around
the corner, had yet to stake its claim.

The bare shoulder hunches up to involuntary rectitude.
Even at the beach your trained body slips

to attention. Your cocky squint
and Elvis sneer exude detached

experience, a ruse learned
at military school to bluff your wardens.

The tot (myself) on father's lap
is also detached.

Her eyes are only for you, Sweet Foreign Sibling,
Exotic American.

She reaches for your soldier hand,
but there's no reach back.

It's her first—and only—shot
at unrequited love, the earliest taste of exile.

Precocious pretty-boy flirt, little
homme fatal standing frigid—here, yet

away, alone—overexposed, uniformed
in braided blue, graduated, 'grown up,'

did you sense, then, what lay ahead?
Seduction and betrayal and then again the pitch,

a dynamic so familiar
it almost felt like home.

And then the biggest lie, the Saigon saga,
the drugs and drink to swallow it all.

The others pose for the camera,
competitive in their obedience,

but we, my still distant brother,
resist their matching Cheshire grins.

Our Ava Gardner mother flashes her Hollywood smile,
glamour-plated, seductive, calculating.

She leans over us, connects with the camera,
pulls us toward the lens with her greedy eyes.

Her husband, pasty-white, complicit
in a circle of offspring,

cradles the plump sweetness on his lap,
final issue of his fertile heart, while the others strain,

maintaining the flex of their cheeks—just so—
charming the available light.

Mantilla

Paper-thin prayer thing,
neither shawl nor veil nor scarf nor cape:
swaddler of babes and believers:
to leave you is to grow up.
I loved being swaddled
in your black and pearl gray lace,
such womanly colors for a preteen who received
you as a keepsake from her mother
on a trip to Spain, each tiny knot in the cloth
pulled tight
by some bent-over crone in a rocker
in the Canary Islands or sullen Andalusía.

We fingered the mantillas in the box,
leafing through them like a book,
speed-reading for fineness of texture
and design, proportion and holy aspect,
that day we walked on the Gran Via, two
pious knockouts—*como hermanas se parecen*—
shopping for church garments, head coverings
to wear to Mass, long gauzy shimmer
draped over our bare shoulders
so as not to offend saints, or arouse priests.

See how I profane your lace, pull it
around my neck in a jocular noose-knot,
its anarchy of frills bursting from my staid collar
in funky irreverence,
a flourish to amuse our grown-up son,
whom we will meet
for lunch
at Hattie's
if he'll have us.

The knot at my neck—
It's not irrelevant. I remember now.
It has a sacred, insubstantial use.
I tied it loose
to remind myself to pray—only tentatively—
not to presume,
not even to hope.

Transition: Inheriting Maps

Remember the maps, Father,
the ones we rescued
from the great purge
of papers and books
that day we moved you?
Maps from around the world,
souvenirs of our shared past.

Together at the filing cabinet—
you on the stool, I bending over you—
both of us straining to see without glasses,
measuring memory against grid,
matching history with place,
locating the whereness and whatness
of the intransitive *was*—

without object or home,
united in the grammar of common
longing, reaching back together
for clarity, pattern, design—as if life
could be surveyed with tripod and transit,
angles and distance
define the faultlines, account for time.

The years reveal themselves in maps:
Port Harcourt, Pakambaru,
Tripoli—petroleum cities by now
obliterated—unfold their spectral
streets to us, provide transitory homes
for the careless American diaspora.
Oil under it all.

Imperial, enchanted childhood!

Crude spurts up through the page,
staining present, blurring past,
the tanker at the dock
now in relief, Father's pipeline
unloaded, stretched out
across island, desert, harbor.

The box of maps spills
over with postcards and travel
brochures, snapshots of
Assam the gardener grinning
his fan-tooth smile,
Sunday and Uden and Marta
in paper white uniforms, serving,
always serving brats and bosses
on three continents
forever.

The veined paper stretches
out between us, its red
and blue pulsing with codes
we both would decipher,
longitude and latitude obscurely
circumscribing the real:

your freckled arm reaches for mine,
the mottled skin my legend,
bent arthritic finger my future.

My still strong hand receives
the maps, appropriates the legacy, as
you prepare for the next transfer.

Abanico Habanero

para mi madre

No you said, with a snap of the wrist,
not the first.
There was never a first fan.

A tug at the tattered folds reveals an Asian cliché:
watery pond, mountains, misty trees,
generic reeds brushing up in the wind.
A strip of painted muslin binds twenty skinny sticks
carved of scentless sandalwood.
At the base, an ivory ring.

And hanging from the ring like
a graduate's tassel, a dozen silk strands,
shabby yellow remnant of the wagging tail
that once tickled me as it pumped for breeze.

You correct me from your hospital bed,
a frail bird propped by pillows. Stuck
in the nest, past magnificence,
memory doing the final work of living.
We always had fans, the way we always had shoes.
From China.
Never from Cuba.

My first fan, the one *I* remember, was long
as my arm and definitely Cuban,
a grown-up feminine defense
against tropical heat, flapped
with flamenco severity to conceal
or reveal
a coquette smile.

Now its stand-in fits in my hand like a toy.
Banal landscape bleeding through its verso,
lines of the past too faint to read.

I assist you gingerly, lift you to your regimen,
fold and unfold you in your sick bed.
Your bones crack like twigs, refuse
to bend with the burden of skin, an armature
tired of the form it supports. It bucks its protest,
snapping your vertebrae to register its point. One, then two
breaks, then the pelvis for good measure.

I want to yield to its force, help you make the final break.
But the halfhearted heart beats its wing-beat answer
not yet, not yet—
like your brother Lelén zipping back from his first heart attack
shouting to Caballero, the undertaker, waving
from his funeral parlor: *¡Todavía no!*

Your spine winds to its base,
brittle as a snake's molting,
support gone; only the carapace remains. That
and the ambivalent will.
Still, you heal.

In Cuba the sign for a fork in the road is a fan:
rays spread out like a card hand,
flicking out and in,
ida y vuelta,
paths converging on a single point.

Havana fan,
abanico Habanero,
Habanera—
Mamá—
Old flirt, old worn-out glamour puss,
old peacock's tail,
ancient ornament, you turn to dust in my hand.

II
DEPOSITION

I.

Before Losing You at the Market, Finding You in the Temple

Summer nights at the souk: jugglers and hucksters,
vendors boiling at their stands,
the three of us hand in hand, cranky from the heat.

My grip on you would loosen and you'd break
away, then come back, then be off again,
appraising the *tchotchkes*, chatting up merchants.

You were like that, affable beyond reason,
little god enrobed in light, diving
into the crowd, riding it like a wave,

and we the pathetic shore
awaiting you, diminished
by every foray, consoled by the returns, until

we were the thinnest
sliver of beach
imaginable,

and you—
you were the sea.

2.

The Effects of Intemperance

—*after Jan Steen*

It's the usual story, the mother has fallen asleep, too bored
And exhausted to notice what is happening around her.
All the lights in the house on: TVs, computers, radios
Alive with violence and sex; the children—mine,
But not mine—
Running around naked,
Shouting casual obscenities,
Laughing the careless laugh
Of the young.
A pig presides in the center
In a manger full of straw, and before him,
As in a nativity scene,
Parade the lusty children
Heralding him with roses
As they grab each other's pricks
And romp.

The parrot on his perch
Repeats their chant:
Hail the pig! Hail the pig!
Hail the pig!

I am dreaming the dream of helpless inattention.
The pig is real.

3.

Sacra Conversazione

We're at the gates of the temple.
The arch of the portico, the reliefs on the columns
give away the period.

Your father and I are dressed
in robes of opulent brocade
too elegant, really,

for a carpenter and his wife.
From your place on the steps
you look straight out the picture frame,

brazen and unafraid, chin defiant on your fiddle.
I think, oh, he must be the artist,
doing that Renaissance self-portrait thing.

Suddenly you swing around,
urgent and certain,
I have something to say to you—

But we are talking and talking
as usual while Saint Peter hovers
at the threshold.

His keys' hypnotic glint
catches your eye, beckoning.
You put down your instrument,

say what you have to say,
walk to the other side, step
into the realm where we are not.

Only your echo remains:
I am not like you. I am not like you.
I am not like you.

4.

Annunciation

In our version your father kneels beside me
on the receding checkered tiles,
waiting to receive the news.

You float before us, raiment billowing,
your long boyhood curls
blond and bright as lightning.

I am praying the usual prayer,
something about protecting you
from illness or danger.

Your words travel their diagonal trajectory
like a bullet
into my ear, through my brain, into

my bloodstream. My womb quickens.
What was only dread has
taken up residence.

I am not full of grace.
I am not blessed among women.

5.

Palm Sunday

I'm the one riding the donkey
you and your father flank my sides

I am not wearing a crown
I am not Queen of the Happy Few

all Jerusalem is in the streets
Muslim and Jew alike wailing at the Wailing Wall

it's one of those Mannerist scenes
the indifferent mass swarms the canvas

while the three of us play out our private drama
in a tiny corner, almost offstage

no one cares about our turmoil or discord
I hold a scepter made of palms

good: I can live with this

6.

Agony in the Garden

At supper he whispers something in your ear,
the Judas boy, who wants you.

We go to the garden where it's cool
and wait.

From my place against the tree
I see you through the window,

watch as you walk from door to desk,
reach into your pocket,

pull out your wallet, empty it and leave it by the lamp,
pick up a pen, lean over to write, then don't,

take something heavy from the drawer, put it back
then sweep the money into a paper bag.

You walk from desk to door and out, your hand
reaching back to put out the light.

On the security film you leave the building
alone, holding the heavy bag.

Off camera you walk towards the Charles, leave
your saddle shoes under the pedestrian bridge.

We wait in the garden.
And wait.

We don't know yet whom you meet or why.
We don't know yet that the river has claimed you.

7.

Deposition

I am in the foreground in mid-swoon, still reeling,
red cloak blown open in the sudden storm.
Darkness obscures the horizon and behind me

a construction site, men on a ladder, the fence
which became your cross—and behind the fence
a church spire

blessing nothing. The sword
I have always known would pierce my heart
cuts through me.

The young corpse slung
over your father's friend and namesake
is yours.

The pasty boy-flesh stark
against the weathered arms bearing you
is yours.

My women friends are all named Mary. They lean into me,
murmuring Aramaic consolations. Bent in sorrow,
they catch my fall.

A column of light pans the scene from above.
The vast Wyoming sky bursts
with a waterless electric rain.

The Palladian arch framing the scene
contains my grief.
That's how I know this is a dream.

8.

The Bad Thief is a Mother

She hangs to his left, howling obscenities
to the wind.

She schemed and stole
for her son,

for him alone explored
the devil's neighborhood,

flirted with bureaucrats,
made deals with principals,

winked at her own accommodations,
the familiars she'd found in lies.

Now the ultimate lie:
she has no regrets.

Fact: there's nothing left for her to do
but hang there

and curse.

9.

Pietà

This time the migraine came with a vision
bathed in night sweat:

I was sitting on the Eames chair,
your man's body on my lap, legs

and arms white as casein draped over
mine, spilling onto the cassock, new sores

on your legs, dried blood
on your feet and hands,

from your chalk mouth
the words *forgive me,*

from mine, the impossible
no

10.

Cup

There you are again, arms
outstretched as if to welcome me.

I am fluttering
in the arc of space between your elbow and hip.

Your blood is a river from your side; tributaries
flow from your hands and feet.

I am the sorcerer's apprentice trying to catch the flood,
catch it in my shallow cup, but the cup fills and overflows

and I am exposed as again
failing you.

The others are better at this work of blood-gathering;
one cocksure *putto* even naps on the job.

Sure of his miraculous vessel, he dozes on a wing,
while the promise is

fulfilled.
I cannot meet your faltering stare.

My fathomless shame as I shrink
when you say

Now drink!

I I .

Judgment Day

—after Luca Signorelli

Our eager bodies pull through a sea of dirt
to join their tranquil souls—

your father and I
together in the same grave.

The other soul we seek is yours; we can't relax,
we think, on this raft of Afterlife, until we find it.

We notice without shame that we are naked, and that our naked bodies
are hairless (which we like) and sexless (which we don't).

We look everywhere, turn up earth mounds and stones,
but slowly boredom overcomes us, and we stop.

Anxiety numbs, perception clouds:
we vaguely notice that the rubble around us

resembles a Jewish cemetery somewhere,
jumble of gravestones and history just beyond reach.

It occurs to us in our fog that you might be among the damned,
but that thought is too strenuous to maintain,

too heavy for our ever lighter beings to carry
in this erasure of Everafter,

as are all the worries of you, the vitality of
daily fear, the eternal

madness of parenthood which turns out
not to be eternal.

All that is indelible fades.
The oblivion of the saved is their damnation.

12.

Lamentation

You are sitting on a bed of rosemary, head cocked
In my direction,
Your antlers a forest of gold,

Red underpaint showing through in fine veins.
You are Memory and Loss.
You are Mourning.

You are the Queen's mythic pet
Afloat on a bed of herbs.
To your right my Virgin robes brush

The forget-me-nots, invisible
Feet crushing the maidenhair.
I am listless today. My agony's spent.

The fruit of my womb
Has fallen afar; I have filled
A vase with speedwell and adonis

To no avail.
I have rubbed my aching heart with arnica.
I look to you for solace.

The long-stemmed roses have been cut
And strewn about face down, for modesty.
I am drying the violets for later consolation.

What more can I do?
You are a white hart afloat on a bed of rosemary.

13.
Genuine Repose During the Flight from Egypt

It was the old sleep that came over me.
Old, as in *old soul*.

It was the sleep that had been around, burned
through both testaments, and finally settled down
to nest on my breast.

It was the sleep for which I had been waiting
and which had been waiting for me,

waiting for the body to give in, stop
running away, hiding
under the familiar tasks and stresses,

sweeping up the sawdust, beating my tunic
against the river rocks,
keeping up with the race.

It was the sleep of angels
that comes over you like a lead apron,

settles in on your vulnerable organs and says
rest, tomorrow you will resume your fugitive pace.
In my sleep I answered in the tongue of my infancy

no te vayas, Sueño
Viejo—
but by dawn it was gone.

14.

Catch

Again I'm Veronica chasing you, desperate
To be of service. You are dead-set
On your mission, unwavering in your path.

We're in one of those tapestries
With scenes of the Passion from left to right,
The sky a turquoise mass of undulating waves.

Your skin of silver thread is bleeding
Ruby droplets, your pallor
Radiant in the silken sun.

Your humanity is slipping away, fated
As the seasons, as you move upwards,
Molting toward heaven. I reach

To blot your face but the cloth
Catches on a thorn. I want
To loosen the crown, cover

Your brow with kisses, say
It's going to be all right.
But you look away, resume your work.

Someone hands me back my veil.
I watch the imprint emerge
Slow as a Polaroid.

But the face that looks back at me is not yours.
The face I must face is mine.

III

Time Orders Old Age to Destroy Beauty

The crone has come.
I've seen her before. First,
as a Rubens madam, holding
the light to Delilah and her barber
castrating Samson with a haircut, each fallen tress
pulling her gap-toothed smile a little wider.

Once in a procession of shepherdesses
in an adoration scene by an unknown Neapolitan,
she hovered on the hillside licking her chops.

I know her, too, from Leonardo's sketches,
each sepia line a record of some love lost or
never won, her face a map of disappointment.

Recently I found her in the painting by Pompeo
Girolamo Batoni, obscure but potent on the museum wall.
She is haggard but muscular, unashamed
of her bare shoulders, her gooseflesh neck
twisting as she reaches for the kill.

Though old, she is vigorous in obeying
orders. From the shadows she yanks in
the dark like a stage curtain, whips
out her craggy arm, swipes at the still
pretty lady in late career.
The crone has come.

Bitch Diary

Porco cane! Another day breaks
with a gun shot and a chorus
of yelping bloodhounds after boar.

I ache to join in, but stay quiet, loyal
dog-pig that I am. Pig-dog.
Purebred cur in a pen: *Sono io.*

The hunt's trained out of me.
Bark and growl, the baser instincts,
I renounced them long ago.

My tail springs up
like an erection
at the smell of animal,

but the chase
is forbidden. Always,
my inner *down girl!*

prevails. It never fails.
Not for me the bait of barnyard cats
and wild-goose foxes. I know

not to waste *my* nose
on vulgar game
or public sport.

I save myself
for the hidden
and vegetal.

I stalk the peculiar scent, wave
my tail like a secret banner when I catch the smell,
and follow the musk in silence

with a steady walk
to the still,
earthbound thing.

I paw the surface for a sign
—root-mold, fungus, spore—
then dig and claw

just to the tip of the tuber
till desire trumps dirt and
I lift the truffle.

I keep my panting discreet
and always deliver.
God, I am one good dog.

My mantra: Abhor blood.
Leave the surface to others;
dwell in the underworld.

Pentecost: Waiting

It's not like you to sit so high in a marble throne,
encrusted with pearls, no less.

Your acolytes in the circle below puzzle at your sudden
distance and wait for initiation into the sacred mysteries.

We're in that recurring workshop dream,
the one where expectations are vague until disappointment clarifies.

We are waiting, a banner explains
in gold heraldic script,

for the cloven tongues
like as fire, for the spirit to give us utterance.

Confident monolith—frontal, iconic—
fingertips touching as if in prayer, you

fix your gilt metal gaze on the silky dove above, its
twelve winged seraphim hovering in attendance.

The tortoise, the dog and the roebuck mock
us from the garden. The peacock and the lily concur.

Rose petals shower down from the basilica dome.
No flames descend to light on our heads.

Forty Days

—*after Hieronymous Bosch*

I am the desert,
        incubus of change raining all over me.
Fish ape doves in a radium sky, and I—
        I am choking for air.

Surpliced chimps ride curates in feathers while
        the alabaster lizard man tempts me
to his perch. Hands and tongue tease off my habit, limbs
        spread their scales to enfold me—

I recoil
        then succumb,
repent—
        and want him again.

I am bored with inexorable cycles.
        Desire. Ravishment.
Regret. From sainthood
        to sinner and back.

Help me decipher
        the words on the bird-rat's beak. Teach
me to swallow the spit of the griffin and take
        the embrace of the spectacled snake.

Sweet demon, hand
        me your tail, guide
me to the glass chamber in the garden,
        the roiling center

where spirit and flesh mingle
        in a brackish elixir.
Leave me to stew
        in the pastel vortex,

study the whirlwind, read
        meaning in the punishing heat, burn
in the current, record it
        and not be consumed.

CPSIA information can be obtained at www.ICGtesting.com
Printed in the USA
LVOW05s1327181114

414320LV00009B/159/P

9 780226 069678